Eileen

Women

Compiled by
Evelyn L. Beilenson

PETER PAUPER PRESS, INC.
WHITE PLAINS · NEW YORK

Thanks to Laura Kuczma for editorial assistance.

Copyright © 1991
Peter Pauper Press, Inc.
202 Mamaroneck Avenue
White Plains, NY 10601
ISBN 0-88088-748-6
Printed in Hong Kong
5   4

WOMEN

No laborer in the world is expected to work for room, board, and love—except the housewife.

Letty Cottin Pogrebin

I used to be snow-white . . . but I drifted.

Mae West

Keep fit—but not for your
men. Do it for yourselves.

Jane Fonda

Childbirth is more admirable
than conquest, more amazing
than self-defense, and as
courageous as either one.

Gloria Steinem

Whether women are better
than men I cannot say—but I
can say they are certainly no
worse.

Golda Meir

Losing my virginity was a
career move.

Madonna

I married the first man I ever kissed. When I tell my children that, they just about throw up.

Barbara Bush

It is a truth universally acknowledged that a single man in possession of a good fortune must be in want of a wife.

Jane Austen
Pride and Prejudice

Marriage may have turned into
a junk bond. But nothing is so
romantic as a risk.

Tracy Young

There is a myth that if you
amass enough wealth, then
your life falls into place.

Helen Hunt

Lost time was like a run in a
stocking. It always got worse.
Anne Morrow Lindbergh

Even if something is left
undone, everyone must take
time to sit still and watch the
leaves turn.
Elizabeth Lawrence

Conversation between Adam and Eve must have been difficult at times—they had nobody to talk about.

Agnes Repplier

Women and elephants never forget.

Dorothy Parker

For years [my wedding ring]
has done its job. It has led me
not into temptation. It has
reminded my husband numer-
ous times at parties that it's
time to go home. It has been a
source of relief to a dinner
companion. It has been a
status symbol in the maternity
ward.

Erma Bombeck

If men could get pregnant,
abortion would be a sacrament.

Florynce Kennedy

If you're going to be able to
look back on something and
laugh about it, you might as
well laugh about it now.

Marie Osmond

Women's propensity to share
confidences is universal. We
confirm our reality by sharing.
Barbara Grizzuti Harrison

To deny we need and want
power is to deny that we hope
to be effective.

Liz Smith

The main problem in marriage
is that, for a man, sex is a
hunger—like eating. If a man
is hungry and can't get to a
fancy French restaurant, he'll
go to a hot dog stand. For a
woman, what's important is
love and romance.

Joan Fontaine

Let Greeks be Greeks, and
women what they are.

Anne Bradstreet

A woman of honor should never suspect another of things she would not do herself.

Marguerite de Valois

There are no more thorough prudes than those women who have some little secret to hide.

George Sand

Marriage is a great institution,
but I'm not ready for an
institution, yet.

Mae West

It takes a woman twenty years
to make a man of her son, and
another woman twenty minutes
to make a fool of him.

Helen Rowland

If truth is beauty, how come
no one has their hair done in a
library?

Lily Tomlin

You don't have to make a
decision when you're eighteen
about what you're going to do
when you're fifty, but you do
need to keep your options
open.

Jean Auel

[Dorothy Thompson is] the
only woman in history who
has had her menopause in
public and made it pay.
Alice Roosevelt Longworth

After ecstasy, the laundry.
Zen statement

To be happy with a man you must understand him a lot and love him a little. To be happy with a woman you must love her a lot and not try to understand her at all.

Helen Rowland

I love men, not because they are men, but because they are not women.

Christina, Queen of Sweden

Women prefer men who have
something tender about them—
especially the legal kind.

Kay Ingram

My success was not based so
much on any great intelligence
but on great common sense.

Helen Gurley Brown

As women we have to define
power in our own terms and
use power to achieve a better
life for women, children and
all citizens.

Nita Lowey

I think men and women have a
sort of obligation between
them to make life attractive
and picturesque.

Katharine Hepburn

If the women's movement did
any harm at all, it gave the
woman who stayed at home an
inferiority complex.
Barbara Walters

A gentleman is a patient wolf.
Henrietta Tiarks

But I don't believe women
ever get sensible, not even
through prolonged association
with their husbands.

Dorothy L. Sayers

Don't compromise yourself.
You are all you've got.

Betty Ford

Some men are so macho they'll get you pregnant just to kill a rabbit.

Maureen Murphy

You have to decide at the end of the day if you can live with yourself.

Princess Anne,
on her work with
Third World children

I don't think of all the misery
but of the beauty that still
remains.

Anne Frank

Perhaps nature is our best
assurance of immortality.

Eleanor Roosevelt

When a woman ceases to alter the fashion of her hair, you guess that she has passed the crisis of her experience.

Mary Austin

The feminist movement—the glorious perception that women can be valued for our brains and not just for our faces—makes it possible for a woman to become 50 and not to grieve.

Karen DeCrow

New York City has finally hired women to pick up the garbage, which makes sense to me, since, as I've discovered, a good bit of being a woman consists of picking up garbage.

Anna Quindlen

My personal life has nothing to do with my ability. You, as an individual, are the only one who has control over your image.

Paula Zahn

I don't find it hard to understand why a woman stays in a marriage when she is being beaten. When you come into a relationship with that amount of self-hate, hitting becomes a warped form of affection.

Mariette Hartley

The power I exert on the court depends on the power of my arguments, not on my gender.

Justice Sandra Day O'Connor

A woman can not guarantee
her heart, even though her
husband be the greatest and
most perfect of men.

George Sand

I feel very adventurous. There
are so many doors to be
opened, and I'm not afraid to
look behind them.

Elizabeth Taylor,
on being single again

All too many men still seem to believe, in a rather naive and egocentric way, that what feels good to them is automatically what feels good to women.

Shere Hite

Many women have more power than they recognize, and they're very hesitant to use it, for they fear they won't be loved.

Patricia Schroeder

A woman must have money
and a room of her own.

Virginia Woolf

I never used words like "sexy"
in the '20s. To me, that was
like talking about toilets. I
preferred to use words like
"romantic" when a man sent
flowers or poems.

Gloria Swanson

When I started modeling, it was one of the few fields where a woman could make money. But those days are gone forever. Women are no longer being kept on the back burner. There are going to be lots of superstars.

Lauren Hutton

Never go to bed mad. Stay up and fight.

Phyllis Diller

The reason husbands and wives do not understand each other is because they belong to different sexes.

Dorothy Dix

I always read the last page of a book first so that if I die before I finish I'll know how it turned out.

Nora Ephron

My advice is marry the
"wrong" person with the right
kinds of feelings and have a
wonderful adventure!

Mary Douthit,
after 37 years of marriage

A well-kept house is the sign
of a misspent life.

Kitchen Plaque

When you cease to make a
contribution you begin to die.
Eleanor Roosevelt

The two key issues for women
in the 1990s and beyond will
be affordable and dependable
childcare and breaking through
the glass ceiling of corporate
America.

Lillian Vernon

Sex is a fortuitous discovery,
the more so, I suppose, if one
comes to it late. But perhaps
those who feel this compulsive
urge to lay their discoveries on
the rest of us could get
together in confession clubs
and leave us to our private
pleasurings, all variations of
which had been discovered,
surely, well before the advent
of the wheel.

Martha Weinman Lear

People always have a comment to make and it used to really bother me, "Your skirts are too short, your skirts are too long. Do this with your hair, do that with your hair. . . ." Comments you'd never make to a man about his bald spot. No one would ever go up to a man and say "You should have a hair transplant."

Dianne Feinstein

I praise loudly; I blame softly.

Catherine II of Russia

Women want to read about glamour. They have their problems. They want to see the fantasy. I've lived that life. What other women dream about I have lived.

Ivana Trump

I'm not denyin' the women are
foolish: God Almighty made
'em to match the men.

George Eliot,
Adam Bede

Never lend your car to anyone
to whom you have given birth.

Erma Bombeck

The best advice yet given is
that you don't have to take it.

Libbie Fudim

How can I choose a husband
when I can't even decide what
to wear?

Beth Jaykus

I have a simple philosophy.
Fill what's empty. Empty
what's full. And scratch where
it itches.

Alice Roosevelt Longworth

There is no scientific answer
for success. You can't define it.
You've simply got to live it and
do it.

Anita Roddick

The qualities of our later life
will be determined by the life
we have already shaped.

Rose Kennedy

If you want to sacrifice the
admiration of many men for
the criticism of one, go ahead,
get married.

Katharine Hepburn

It's a waste of time trying to
change a man's character. You
have to accept your husband
as he is.

Queen Elizabeth II

Whatever else can be said
about sex, it cannot be called a
dignified performance.

Helen Lawrenson

Women complain about sex
more often than men. Their
gripes fall into two major
categories: (1) Not enough.
(2) Too much.

Ann Landers

Every cook would be more
imaginative if they were not
catering for people!

Pam Brown

Your success and happiness lie in you.

Helen Keller

Even a stopped clock is right twice a day.

Marie Ebner-Eschenbach

I climbed the ladder of success
wrong by wrong.
Patricia Brooks

Don't accept rides from strange
men—and remember that all
men are strange as hell.
Robin Morgan

Power is the ability to make change.

Geneva Overholser

Marriage is not just spiritual communion and passionate embraces; marriage is also three-meals-a-day and remembering to carry out the trash.

Joyce Brothers

Having it all doesn't necessarily
mean having it all at once.
Stephanie Luetkehans

Dressing up for me is not an
effort. And if you live with
someone, it's a courtesy to
look as good as you can.
Paloma Picasso

By and large, mothers and housewives are the only workers who do not have regular time off. They are the great vacationless class.

Anne Morrow Lindbergh

Women are the glue that holds our day-to-day world together.

Anna Quindlen

Men of sense in all ages abhor
those customs which treat us
only as the vassals of your sex.
Abigail Adams

If men got pregnant, there
would be safe, reliable methods
of birth control. They'd be
inexpensive, too.
Anna Quindlen

Pretty women are like
sovereigns: one flatters them
only through self-interest.

Madame de Staël

Women love always: when
earth slips from them, they
take refuge in heaven.

George Sand

"Who inu hell," I said to
myself, "wants to try to make
pies like Mother makes when
it's so much simpler to let
Mother make um inu first
place?"

Harriette Arnow

I enjoy dating married men
because they don't want
anything kinky, like breakfast.
Joni Rodgers

Men and women, women and men. It will never work.

Erica Jong

A lady is one who never shows her underwear unintentionally.

Lillian Day

A wise woman puts a grain of
sugar into everything she says
to a man, and takes a grain of
salt with everything he says to
her.

Helen Rowland

My mother was raised with a
terror of touching, which left
me feeling needy and
unfulfilled.

Mariette Hartley

I don't want to make money. I just want to be wonderful.
Marilyn Monroe

I'm tired of all this nonsense about beauty being only skin-deep. That's enough. What do you want, an adorable pancreas?
Jean Kerr

Noncooks think it's silly to invest two hours' work in two minutes' enjoyment; but if cooking is evanescent, well, so is the ballet.

Julia Child

If you stand up for yourself and you're a man, they admire you. If you stand up for yourself and you're a woman, they call you a bitch.

Bette Davis

Whenever you see food
beautifully arranged on a
plate, you know someone's
fingers have been all over it.

Julia Child

Be bold in what you stand for
and careful what you fall for.

Ruth Boorstin

As I grow older, I become
more and more of a Marxist—
Groucho, that is. When you
have lived two-thirds of your
life, you know the value of a
good joke.

Karen DeCrow

A liberated woman is one who
has sex before marriage and a
job after.

Gloria Steinem

When I was a little girl, I
loved Halloween because it
was the only day of the year
when I was beautiful.
                    Anna Quindlen

As a woman, I'm realistic
about the fact I still have to
mix toughness and femininity
to be accepted.
                    Sheila Stainback

Men are brought up to
command, women to seduce.
                    Sally Kempton

It makes me angry to think
that . . . female sanitation
workers will spend their days
doing a job most of their co-
workers think they can't
handle, and then they will go
home and do another job most
of their co-workers don't want.
                    Anna Quindlen

I know I have the body of a
weak and feeble woman, but I
have the heart and stomach of
a king, and of a king of
England too.

Queen Elizabeth I

Success to me is having ten
honeydew melons and eating
only the top half of each one.

Barbara Streisand

In the 1990s and beyond, I
imagine a world less informed
by the competitive and hier-
archical structures which
characterize our male-built
society, a world which
recognizes complexity of truths
and individual differences—
infinite refractions of the
divine image.

Rabbi Shira Milgrom

If you haven't got anything
nice to say about anybody,
come sit next to me.
          Alice Roosevelt Longworth

Nobody wants to kiss when
they are hungry.
          Attributed to *Dorothy Dix*

For most of my life the only
ceremonies I've been to at
which women were the stars
were weddings. So I like
weddings.

Anna Quindlen

Women may be the one group
that grows more radical with
age.

Gloria Steinem

What I consider my weaknesses
are feminine traits: incapacity
to destroy, ineffectualness in
battle.

Anaïs Nin

The pedigree of honey
Does not concern the bee;
A clover, any time, to him
Is aristocracy.

Emily Dickinson

While forbidden fruit is said
to taste sweeter, it usually
spoils faster.

Abigail Van Buren

Sex appeal is 50 percent what
you've got and 50 percent
what people think you've got.

Sophia Loren

Never mistake knowledge for wisdom. One helps you make a living; the other helps you make a life.

Sandra Carey

I was happier in the air than on the ground. I probably always will be.

Mary Martin

The sharing of food is the
basis of social life, and to
many people it is the only
kind of social life worth
participating in.

Laurie Colwin

We are tomorrow's past.

Mary Webb

Love is like the wild-rose briar;
  Friendship is like the
  holly-tree.
The holly is dark when
the rose briar blooms,
  But which will bloom
  most constantly?

Emily Brontë

Never eat more than you can
lift.

Miss Piggy

My only sketch, profile, of
Heaven is a large blue sky, and
larger than the biggest I have
seen in June—and in it are my
friends—every one of them.

Emily Dickinson

It's been a fabulous life and a
wonderful career. I'll keep
living until it's time. Then I'll
just go on to another stage.

Mary Martin